AFTER IMAGE

Charles Borkhuis

chax press 2006

ISBN 0-925904-60-0

The author gratefully acknowledges the following publications in which poems in *Afterimage* first appeared:

First Intensity 20 – 2005 (ed. Lee Chapman)
EOAGH – 2006 (ed. Tim Peterson)

Part Three "The Tooth Fairy" was presented as a staged performance in the "Plays on Words Festival" produced by Tony Torn and directed by Mallory Catlett at the Ontological-Hysteric Theater, NYC, on May 12, 2006. Performers: Pete Simpson with Mary Archias, Jessica Jelliffe, Kara Tyler, eth Kurkjian, Katherine Creel, Morgan Pecelli, Livia de Paolis, Gillian Chadsey, and Young Jean Lee.

Cover photo: Ethan Page

Author's headshot: Elliot Page

Special thanks to: Kathleen Page and Kieron Murphy

for Kathleen

AFTERIMAGE

Part One: The Big Picture

Part Two: Friendly Fire

Part Four: Pool Scum

PART ONE

The Big Picture

picture this . . .

her frozen face staring back
like a dead rabbit in a trap

flash

life goes on but the photo is
its own little tomb

maybe she was still alive
outside the snapshot

but nobody escapes for long

look again . . .

nine women in nine windows

turn their clocks back

synchronically

then close their curtains one by one
as the house on stilts
tilts

sand flows red
every time I

turn over the glass
(so much for counting)

someone puts a gun
to your head
and you stop dreaming

wheels screech
and a cap goes off

powder on the brain

rewind the tape
listen closer . . .

there's a dead man talking

who said
nothing's as empty
as an empty pool

no slide into reflection
just more leaves in the drain
no name no time
for any of it
now in the afters
we might encounter and so on
indefinitely
I can't speak about it

someone dives
there is a splash

water overflows
the blinding sun

it is midnight
the pool is empty

she puts her fingers
in my mouth
and feels around

black stones of a cave
my eyes close forever

she has climbed back
into the photo

she is dressed
in a black bathing suit
near the pool

I am in the photo with her
it is dusk
we are standing eye to eye
frozen
in love's momentary flash

what happens after this
slides off the surface
like a viscous film

"go away
go away from here"

her head was still shaking
inside mine

I left and she disappeared
together we made a perfect zero
one thing happens and then another
not necessarily in that order

sure I'm talking in circles
but the tape keeps running
just in case

face it
my eggs always come up
hard-boiled
no matter how long I bubble

sure we're all
silhouettes moving
behind a screen
but certain games grow
a greener shade of mold

looking at my reflection
in the toy store window

my hung over
raccoon eyes
my rubbery red lips

an elderly salesclerk motions
through the glass
once inside I'm handed
a furry dog mask
I squint through tiny eyeholes
at the mirror

"my god" the clerk says
"it's you"

dozed off in the time it takes
to grow a new head

no one with eyes
can see me now

but the future still follows
like the unnamable
collecting at my feet

stopped in the middle
of a white field
snow filling in my footprints
till I leave no trace

I lie down and look up
at the sky that is burying me

my new head
follows you

home through old streets

it is midday
in the blinding sun

locks turn in their tumblers

the door opens
on a scene

to which I keep returning

echo's end
begin again . . .

a little girl
hands me a blue box
I'm the birthday boy
pulling past the ribbons and wrapping
to a small bloody tooth
buried in white tissue

she smiles showing me
the space between her teeth
I want to climb in
but her mom's flash to the retina
goes off like a warning shot's first kiss

I stumble back in sparks
clouds roam through my temples
and the earth turns
in the opposite direction

astrally I rise
for a snack
while the paralyzed sleeper
drools

nothing ever ends
for the last time
there's always another
knock at the door
another clog in the drain

you're on the skids in a room
dreaming of somebody knocking on a door
indeed this has happened before
"come in"

it's nobody you know
it never is

but it's the same setup

this time it's the chinese
delivery boy buzzing
the wrong bell

gag and tie him to the radiator

pack your ghostly belongings
and get out of town

people say something
what is it
what is it worth

they fall in love with people
who let them be in a certain way
who put up with their self-image
let's call it happiness
or existence
whatever

facts – that's the sly you learn to live by
truth – that's the slippage you least expect

cross the street and a messenger
on a bike knocks my teeth out
then hands me a letter
from a dentist who wants
to put me on a case

his wife left him for an oculist
now she can't see straight

coughed up the plot in a hanky

no point in grinding out another one
I prefer to let it all
fall
between my fingers now

why not just meet me
at the "wrecking ball" and we'll
sip a little moonlight
through a straw

trouble is
I'm the invisible enthymeme
in my own argument
I'm the bullet burrowing
through my own head

even when I'm inside her
I'm the outsider

sure sure
only in metaphor
may we touch
that's why there's cigarettes

still one rises from the dead
one has to eat
the dentist must keep drilling . . .

last time I walked out of the ocean
of sullen commuters
my private eye
looked like a million others

woke up
with my teeth in his hands

turning on the overhead
he peered into my open chasm
like a lion tamer under the big top

"sure is empty in here"

new choppers was his game
he would install the hardware
on the house for a favor

gives me the big toothy
and a photo of the oculist
handsome swarthy type
with a light in the middle of his head

"find something on him friend
and I'll . . ."

"hold the gold doc –
just give me the gas
and I'll sleep on it"

PART TWO

Friendly Fire

double-headed lightness
in the waving room

"let us drill down"

parentheses inside parentheses
set to the shine
off a spinning word

a brown watermark spread
across the town
like a dirty little secret

assassin silhouette
cut-out
hole in a tree
sliver of a moon in water weep
for everyone who must become us

behind the stall about to flush
when two suits at the urinals start to unzip

"I'm talking a story the genre can't resist
I'm talking a story that's all genre"

"what about the plot and characters"

"oh they're in it but they're fragments
traces that self erase
or are transformed into repeating voices
shapes patterns puns dreams
and stories within stories"

"sounds like real life –
but what about stars"

"no stars no actors just people off the street
preferably with no names
it'll all be anonymous –
writer producer director –
no one will know who made the film"

"what's it called"

"the big picture"

"sounds like a winner
where do I sign"

they left and I flushed
the form away with the content
six days of creation
overheard in a men's room

everything is itself
and something else

a question of where the mind runs
magnetized to the broken signs
of a certain
covert operation

stopped outside to tie my twinkies
and two sub-zeroes
rolled me down an alley
into the trunk of a continental
and gunned the engine

the oculist looked into my eyes

"I'd like to buy you a drink"

"what's the game"

"you like to gamble – yes
just remember a bullet in the head
beats a full-house – every time"

the dentist's wife entered in tight whites
bent over and tongued
the space between my teeth

"stay on your own side of the fence"

"sure sure but sometimes
my hand sees in the dark I mean
those little flames
at the end of a blind man's touch"

my fingers started leaving
breath-notes on her thigh

"forget that fool –
whack hubby-dearest and I'll screw
a permanent light bulb
into your head"

silence
flooded in black light

held at a mirror's
knifepoint
dissolve into nameless
desires overflowing the building
onto the sidewalk

shirt striped by dirty blinds
slatted no one sees me
peering at the missing

letters on the neon
sign across the street

below me
an ex-boxer pees
on an electric fence
that sparks in the dark

looking into the center
of the eye strikes me
deadly

maybe the image is empty
and all that's left is a shape
ubiquitous geometry
layer over layer in dancing waves

no doubt the exterior
folds into the interior
at the bat of an eye
what lives in the hole hidden by presence
is anybody's guess

somehow I figured
the woman in the photo was down there
but I might have to die to find her

all I know is
flashbulbs keep going off in my eyes
every time I try to bring her back

woman on the phone
woke me out of a bad dream
said she was the oculist's wife
somebody had slapped her silly
and she was ready to spill the beans

she started talking in a scrambled code
I could only decipher as
bad poetry

something about the
river overflowing its banks
and checks written across the waves
to dead men still alive on the books

someone else was cashing in
on their better halves
yada yada yada . . .
sounded like a movie I'd already seen

I must have fallen back asleep
when I heard her scream
I opened my eyes
and the line went dead

sure sure
water seeks its own level
and arms and legs break
into matchsticks
when the boys uptown give the word

but that didn't explain
the three stoic strangers in raincoats
staring into my hotel window

each turned a page of his pad
synchronically
and continued taking notes

power always has another
spectacle waiting in the wings
where the *little people* gather
to prop up the cardboard scenery

drill down deeper
and the rings go all the way
to the empty center

the hotel lobby featured
an upside down eden
hanging from a peeling
ceiling

bellhops in wrong size uniforms
and white sox
picked pizza from the gold in their teeth
and jingled loose change

insomnia walk with me
through the wee morning hours

where a rippling body
gives me that lost fisheye gaze
from the bottom of the pool

his face was always in the papers
one of the big boys from uptown
that walk on water
downtown wasn't his element

course the body disappeared
before the dicks arrived
lucky I took a polaroid
for my collection

mystery remains in little things
that don't add up
I kept reshuffling the photos
like a deck of cards

the mirror over the fireplace

the knife in a block of cheese

the framed photo of a smiling couple at the beach

the rope on the seat of the pickup

the stopped bedroom clock

the loaded revolver in the underwear drawer

sifting through leftover images
till a passing wing
lends its signature to roving thoughts

pre-flight instructions
pass across dark pupils in a white
dot matrix

big city overload

every somebody needs at least
a 1000 nobodies just to get a leg up

gravity of the situation . . .
I could disappear here
on the periphery

blind spot
stalking my every move

these days I keep my mouth shut
and my old teeth on a chain
those shrunken heads
hanging around my neck
are a daily reminder
of existential decay

ok call me mr. perturbation
but how can I be sure
my new choppers aren't bugged
and the dentist isn't listening in
on every word I say

lift an eyelid up her skirt
as the waitress bends
to tie her laces
I catch her eye watching mine
in the mirror
tattoos of twisting chains
down each arm
stop at her wrists

"refill mr."

story muscle twitch
mr. bubbles and the fish
I smile and she pours
brushing one of her twin peaks
across my cheek

red circumspect lips
signal a secret subway kiss
but neither of us moves
I pop off a shot of her tattoos
just to pacify the worms of plot
as the ex-boxer slides onto the next stool

"keep your eyes on the java cowboy
or you'll be back in the dentist's chair
faster than you can say *beef jerky*"

when my eyes close . . .

I see shoppers
in their underwear riding
up and down
department store escalators
with their somnambulist eyes
and shiny paten leather shoes

everybody's got a false alibi
and another identity or two
squirreled away for a rainy day

photos in the mail
of a politician doing things
to a boy with a half-erased face

scratched off ribbons of surface

you can scroll back a few layers
and hear the screams
but no one's inside those depths

the big picture keeps
slipping out of focus

same sordid slips away
there is money
and there is somebody
who wants to steal it

what's it like
this *dream-jacket*
put it on and I'm another
person in gold buttons
bellhop with a tray on wheels
wandering the halls

yes but and what
may I now
hello room service
did you ever
bring the weather

deep frig full and a heart-shaped
breakfast at eight
tv on your left enjoy your
remote and happy here

now smile a big toothy
and flash your alien palm

"just passing through"

"sure sure isn't everyone"

"yes but . . .
isn't that blood on your fez"

someone is ringing
the servant's bell in my ear

now someone is ringing
the servant's bell in my other ear

I neither rise
nor remain seated

I am neither speaking
nor silent

neither dreaming
nor awake

dead nor alive

PART THREE

The Tooth Fairy

nothing but shadows now
holding up the trees

sell me short
and I'm down the laugh-hole again
with nine women in nine windows
turning their clocks back
to infinity

you get the picture . . .

horse's head on a stick
flying past the dying moon

past the centipede's kick line
on a blade of grass

I'm out of my body all right
but whose body
am I in

narrow spin
down a spiral funnel
to a circular canyon
where I slowly hover
over a pyramidal sand dune . . .

suddenly inside looking up
at the ceiling of a space ship
from what seems strangely
like a dentist's chair

the woman in the photo smiles
inserting something behind my right ear

I'm in love with her all right
but my bridgework keeps pulling me back
to another level

distance decides
what intimacies it can afford

the *next* bubbles over
into the *now*

but I'm too late
to see it coming

too soon
to perceive its departure

pushed the door
wide open

the dentist was drilled
into his swivel chair
by an industrial jackhammer
I stepped into a pool of blood
and tracked it around the office

I'm searching his files for my x-rays
when the dicks burst in
force a birdcage over my head
and apply the locks
then they drop a black cloak
over the contraption
and call it a night

project *squeeze ball*

inferno setup
for a fall-guy wake-up call
prey to cops on the beat
"can't we all just get along"

"I'll ask the questions sonny"
the taste of knuckles
clung to my blood

foaming heads on trees
call me home
tick-tick tick-tick

picture this . . .
eye between my thumb and forefinger
forced *open wide*
for the two-way mirror
(who's on the other side)

slow whispers in the blinding light
"there's a murderer inside you
and we're going to pull him out
like a rotten tooth"

a week without sleep . . .

the cops are your friends
confession frees the soul

same brights day and night

same dripping faucet

shaped like a revolver

same nightstick
raked across your nerves

same questions

same answers

same shit on a shingle

same sinatra tapes
till your mind turns to mousse

staring into solitary . . .
days placed end-on-end
filling up space like child's blocks
that spell out certain words

now I see
the world is composed of blocks
that form shapes with letters written on them

now I see
words floating away from their objects
free to recombine with others

now I see
the letters *a-i-r* written across a table

the chair is spelled *h-o-r-s-e*

the bed is a *b-o-n-e*

the cell is a *b-e-l-l*

now I'm *twelve-thirty*
straight up and down

the hour of my escape

circle drawn upon the wall
where I place my head

sink into the cement
and spin

another kind of drilling . . .

(inside parentheses
detached within a sea of changes)

inhabit the space
between recurrences
between the first and last
distinction and wholeness

neither I nor not-I
but the other's other
whose stare empties me

I can't speak about it
I can only make room for it

end up on the other side

of the wall walking
inside the body of another

across a shaky rope-bridge
between jagged mountain tops

up ahead a sign flashes . . .

"goat's head hotel – two miles"

pitch black out
worms walking the night air
meaning's little minute hand
keeps stroking my face
licking closed lids
a counterfeit truth
leading knowledge
around on a leash

act on what . . .
the vivisection
the sawing of the cage
the pulling back of the ribs
the great void inside
filled with nameless others

am I not going backwards
and forwards in the same breath
who answers in me
but an utter stranger

who is the *not-I* that speaks
in my place

invisible blood

a bald biker with an eye patch
blows smoke in my face
"buy you a beer"
I can see myself
in his stainless steel teeth

a hot number leans over
when I'm not looking and sticks
a needle in my arm

"join the par-ty in twelve thir-ty"

hand over memory
and ankle deep in warm ripples
a piece of sky replaces the bridge
of my nose in the mirror

map drawn across my face
the swollen hills roll under eyelid traces

anyone could take the place
of anyone else now

I'm turning into a woman
or a corpse
the photo has my name attached
but it's peeling off like dead skin

words flap
between the rooms
what they are saying
doesn't apply to me
but who can be sure

the dead have never left
the living are not convinced
they are alive

the mirror has made me
into someone else
they have painted lips on my face
and shadowed my eyes
I am being prepared
for a journey

something walks into my eye
it is never ending

the story has too many holes

I am one of them

I pass through myself

I am not from this place

I am speaking to you
from a future
that will never happen

little girl in a green party dress
holds a dripping candle
near my face . . .

memory's first kiss keeps its glow
basement dartboard overhead
mother's shiny black heels
coming down the stairs

blinding flashlight

"what are you two
doing down there"

. . . the little girl in the hotel hallway
smiles holding out a key
and points to room 1230

unlock the door
and a half-man half-hawk
hands me a flashlight

"nice to see you again
I think you know everyone here"

the moving light caught the guests
squirming like eels
on the bedroom floor
lots of bad breath and exposed organs

the ex-boxer dressed as a hare
was sucking the toes
of the dead man in the pool
only he wasn't dead yet

the three men in raincoats
tied and untied their shoes
while the dentist's wife
spread her tsetse fly wings
and blew the bike messenger
into a cigar-shaped balloon

the oculist in top hat and tux
wore the hind quarters of a cheetah
and peered through binoculars
at nine women in nine windows
slowly peeling grapes

the beast's eye is lowered
on a shade

little monsters
little monsters all around

a library of teeth
come to dinner feast
on the lies that smile
so viciously

sweet confessions spill over dessert
as the waitress's tattooed arms
snake between the plates

"get down on your knees"
the dentist's wife insists

"eat every crumb"

the bellhops keep carrying
more dishes over oily bodies

the politician removes his ten gallon
revealing a bowie knife
growing out of the part in his hair

he aims it at the ace of hearts
affixed to my forehead

sounds of shattering glass
as the moment breaks
into bits

reality check –
someone just bounced

a brick off my head
with an attached photo of me
holding a smoking gun
over the dead man in the pool

the set-up was in full swing
the characters around me
dissolved into the walls
like so many bugs

perhaps I was the murderer after all
but without motive

I could kill and kill again
for no apparent reason

PART FOUR

Pool Scum

dead or alive the same
trace elements
linger at the periphery

the plot thickens but nothing
gets any clearer

except maybe the blind spot
to each point of view

the hollow awareness
of what will never come together
in this or any other lifetime

unless what will never come
is already here
and what has already come
is permanently withheld

each point is everywhere extended
and the same people keep cleaning up

from here you can smell the collapse
into the giant zero
at the core of each moment

the bike messenger
crawled through my window one evening
and left a revolver
near my sleeping ear

"why do you keep
running in place"

maybe we're all on alien strings
walking around
with chips in our heads
from earlier abductions

maybe life's one big game board
and we keep switching roles
like shoes or masks
for the entertainment
of the mother ship

maybe we all wake up
as someone else
or else we never wake up
and just keep making
guest appearances
in each other's dreams

song of the dentist's drill
silent as a missing tooth

the open grave
wet with sleeper's breath
death emptied of escape

the past that never occurred
returns again
hovering between shadows

moon without a face
subjectivity without a subject
I without an "I"
powerless to posit
a way out

silence is a space
between the teeth
through which I crawl

the absence that keeps returning
the absence that never arrives

words fall backwards
like a small avalanche of stones

the sky is a pit
that can never be filled

there was a knock on my shoes
and blood at the door

when I opened it
the dentist's wife rolled her eyes
back to egg whites

she was naked
waving a white flag
with a refrigerator light between her teeth

there was a message
scrawled on the back of the flag . . .

1. you will take the place of someone else

2. you will think his thoughts
   knowing they are not your own

3. you will do reprehensible things
   in the name of the other

4. the knowledge that you are not him
   will remain a secret

5. if you are caught detained and tortured
   it will be the other man who is
   caught detained and tortured

6. if you divulge that you are not the other man
   it is you who will be executed
   while the other man will escape

7. meet me at the pool

it was signed *the dead man*

I closed the book on the dentist's wife
and left through the open window

sometimes the story finds you

inching across midnight
in the messy groundswell of letters

a moist undercover
of rotting leaves

stops me

in the middle of a breath . . .

another dead body on the road

another no one
with anyone's face

the birds had gotten to his eyes

I buried him in the weeds

and kept walking

the crumbling inner world
of the outsider

intermittent weightlessness
hands on floating strings

the bullet that skewers
a million sentiments

nothing is a sufficient cause

everyone is
someone else's
idea of themselves

they burned all the miracles
before we arrived

call-waiting in my coffin
interrupts the laughter of cold-cuts

little birdies in my violin
beating beauty to the punch

death's loose fingers
touch the floating sentence

the politician seated
on the branch of a dead oak turns
he is wearing the head of a hawk

"you can go now
but leave your image with us"

awake in someone's dream . . .

I'm a character staring at a fly
licking his hairy legs

soon a web will find him
and a spider will descend . . .

sneak a mirror's peek
at the politician tied to a chair
I must cleave into his chest
and extract a large tooth
pop the cap and pocket
a fabulous diamond

he says smiling "it's a fake"
burps blood and drops dead

in the wee hours I don my dog mask
drag the politician to the pool
and watch him bubble to the bottom

I want to call for help
but can only bark

besides it's not my part

I must swallow the diamond
get in the car and drive away

somebody kills
and somebody cleans up

we never know each other
just the telephone call
and the clock

the revolver or the mop

am I a murderer
are you a maid

I don't think so

your apology's no good here
it's the pointing finger
that buries a shadow
in my forearm

this one is he and not you
this one is she and not me
here the guilty
there the innocent
here the living
there the dead
this is the door
now I will lock it

your truth is an abomination
a dormant virus waiting for a host
you know better
but are pulled back
history comes with a cost
someone must pay

running for my life
but it all feels like a replay

impenetrable wilderness
turning branch over branch

the moon fills my footprints
with underwater light

sounds of others closing in . . .

a dead man floats
up to these words
as from a bottomless pool

but the words are not his
though he mouths them silently

though he appears in your mirror
he is not you

nor is he your father

nor your father's father

but a faceless falling
through earth and rock
into a vast ocean
between your steps

ubiquitous and unknowable

someone dives . . .

there is a
splash

water overflows
the drowning moon

it is midday
in the blinding sun

the pool is empty

what happens
and what does not happen
are kissing cousins

both exist and do not exist
each inside the other

the woman in the photo
points
to the dead man in the leaves
at the bottom of a dry pool

she could turn her laughter
on and off like a faucet

"so anyone can be replaced
by anyone else" I said

"not quite –
but the same people keep coming back
dressed as total strangers

even you're not the man you seem
but then who is"

"you don't understand
I'm not the murderer in this story"

"then you're the victim
plain and simple"

just then I remembered her –
so *after school friendly* so
in the basement
lights out little girl
behind a blind kiss
wakes up
old beyond her years

somehow I'm a bit player
with a camera
in her middle-age movie

"look" she says pointing
"there's porn scum in the pool"

love elementary as a particle
transformative as a bullet

she grabs her chin and pulls
the skin off her face
the dentist's wife stares back

"the dead walk
rivers between us" she smiles
aiming at my head

I take a flash
before she pulls the trigger

lights out in heaven
dulls the pain to speak subject-less

hold the static in your palm
and breathe
into a brown paper bag

thoughts float to the ceiling
and settle like flies

her thighs open to haunt
the quivering bow
wrap around certitude
slow dance
with an avalanche

deep squeeze my pen dry
shooting volumes
into libraries of sand

so the stars show through
her pantyhose
and the game's played
dirty till I squeal
all the names I've ever known
into a blue velvet glove

where's the shame in going public
I made it all up anyway

by the time you play this tape
I'll be bubbling
at the bottom of a pool
or in a book somewhere
funny how last words
always sound like the first

or is this the sentence
I can't slip out of

dreaming or waking
living or dying
have no limits

the opposites wear masks
what is beyond them
is between them

what we are waiting for
has already arrived
but its not
what we expected

squinting through the eyeholes
of the dog mask

I saw it all
I have the photos
of light crawling under sleepy lids
passing through the eye of a dead man

a naked bulb swings overhead

everyman is his own ghost
but talking about it just draws flies

photo of the first kiss
folded over the last

mother's shiny black heels
on the stairs

"what are you two
doing down there"

blinding flashlight

the speed of the bullet
is equal to the buildup of red sand

the woman in the photo
points to dead leaves
at the bottom of a dry pool

hesitation
at the laugh button

someone is drowning in this picture

About the Author

Charles Borkhuis is a poet, playwright, screenwriter, and essayist. His books of poems are: *Afterimage, Savoir-fear, Alpha Ruins, Dinner with Franz, Proximity (Stolen Arrows), and Hypnogogic Sonnets.* *Alpha Ruins* was selected by Fanny Howe as a finalist for the William Carlos Williams 2001 Book Award. His poems have been anthologized in *Primary Trouble, The Gertrude Stein Awards for Innovative Poetry, Writing From The New Coast, An Avec Sampler #2, The World in Time and Space*, and *Walt Whitman hom(m)age*. His essays on contemporary poetics have appeared in *Telling it Slant* and *We Who Love to Be Astonished,* two books published by the University of Alabama Press. His plays have been presented in NYC, Los Angeles, San Francisco, Hartford, and Paris and published in two collections *Mouth of Shadows and The Sound of Fear Clapping.* His CD, *Black Light*, contains two radio plays produced for NPR and available on www.pennsound. He is the recipient of a Drama-logue Award and the former editor of Theater:Ex, an experimental theater publication. His five recent full-length plays are: *The Man in the Bowler Hat, Dusk, Acting Out, Deep Divide*, and *Escape Velocity.* He is the author of the screenplay "Undercurrent." For the last 15 years, he has curated poetry readings for the Segue Foundation, most recently at Bowery Poetry Club in Manhattan.

Also from Chax Press

Glen Mott, *Analects*
Bruce Andrews, *Swoon Noir*
Joe Amato, *Under Virga*
David Abel, *Black Valentine*
Paul Naylor, *Arranging Nature*
Kass Fleisher, *Accidental Species*
Tenney Nathanson, *Erased Art*
Heather Nagami, *Hostile*
Linh Dinh, *American Tatts*
Patrick Pritchett, *Burn: Doxology for Joan of Arc*
Jonathan Brannen, *Deaccessioned Landscapes*
Beverly Dahlen, *A-Reading Spicer & 18 Sonnets*
Elizabeth Treadwell, *Chantry*

For our many additional titles please visit our web site:
http://www.chax.org/

Chax Press is supported by the Tucson Pima Arts Council and by the Arizona Commission on the Arts with funding from the State of Arizona and the National Endowment for the Arts.

TUCSON PIMA ARTS COUNCIL

Arizona Commission on the Arts

NATIONAL ENDOWMENT FOR THE ARTS